T0266229

Fundamental Issues in Consumption Taxation

David F. Bradford

The AEI Press

Publisher for the American Enterprise Institute

WASHINGTON, D.C.

1996

Although differing slightly in emphasis, this study borrows extensively from "Consumption Taxes: Some Fundamental Transition Issues," in Michael J. Boskin, ed., Frontiers of Tax Reform (Stanford, Calif.: Hoover Institution Press, 1996), pp. 123–50. For help in that paper and its revision I am grateful to Alan Auerbach, Michael Boskin, Niels Frederiksen, Dale Jorgenson, Louis Kaplow, Laurence Kotlikoff, Stephen Moore, Rudolph Penner, Harvey Rosen, Robert Scarborough, Dan Shaviro, Joel Slemrod, Peter Birch Sorensen, Eric Toder, Murray Weidenbaum, and George Zodrow. I would like also to thank the John M. Olin Foundation and Princeton University's Woodrow Wilson School and Center for Economic Policy Studies for supporting my research on tax reform issues. None of these organizations or individuals should be implicated in conclusions expressed herein.

Distributed to the Trade by National Book Network, 15200 NBN Way, Blue Ridge Summit, PA 17214. To order call toll free 1-800-462-6420 or 1-717-794-3800. For all other inquiries please contact the AEI Press, 1150 Seventeenth Street, N.W., Washington, D.C. 20036 or call 1-800-862-5801.

ISBN 0-8447-7068-X
ISBN 978-0-8447-7068-0
1 3 5 7 9 10 8 6 4 2

The AEI PRESS
Publisher for the American Enterprise Institute
1150 17th Street, N.W., Washington, D.C. 20036

Contents

Foreword

Economists, policy makers, and business executives are keenly interested in fundamental tax reform. High marginal tax rates, complex tax provisions, disincentives for saving and investment, and solvency problems in the social security program provide reasons to contemplate how reforms of the tax code and other public policies toward saving and investment might increase economic efficiency, simplify the tax code, and enhance fairness. Many economists believe that gains to the economy from an overhaul of the income tax or from a move to a broad-based consumption tax can be measured in the trillions of dollars. Most conventional economic models indicate a potential for large gains from tax reform.

While many economists agree broadly on the simple analytics of tax reform, they are in much less agreement on such key empirical questions as how much saving or investment would rise in response to a switch to a consumption tax, how much capital accumulation would increase under a partial privatization of social security, how reform would affect the distribution of taxes, and how international capital markets influence the effects of tax reforms in the United States. This lack of professional consensus has made the policy debate fuzzy and confusing.

With these concerns in mind, Diana Furchtgott-Roth and I organized a tax reform seminar series at the

American Enterprise Institute beginning in January 1996. At each seminar, an economist presented new empirical research on topics relating to fundamental tax reform. These topics include transition problems in moving to a consumption tax, the effect of taxation on household saving, distributional effects of consumption taxes in the long and short run, issues in the taxation of financial services, privatizing social security as a fundamental tax reform, international issues in consumption taxation, distributional consequences of reductions in the capital gains tax, effects of tax reform on pension saving and nonpension saving, effects of tax reform on labor supply, consequences of tax reform on business investment, and likely prototypes for fundamental tax reform.

The goal of the pamphlet series in fundamental tax reform is to distribute research on economic issues in tax reform to a broad audience. Each study in the series reflects many insightful comments by seminar participants—economists, attorneys, accountants, and journalists in the tax policy community. Diana and I are especially grateful to the two discussants of each paper, who offered the perspectives of an economist and an attorney.

I would like to thank the American Enterprise Institute for providing financial support for the seminar series and pamphlet series.

R. GLENN HUBBARD
Columbia University

1

Introduction

Motivated by a desire to simplify compliance and improve incentives, many are interested once again in restructuring the U.S. tax system. Most of the proposed reforms would move toward a system based on consumption, rather than income. My purpose in this study is to draw attention to the similarities and differences between the two approaches and to lay out important problems of transition to the consumption-based taxes at the heart of the reform plans.

Four consumption-based reform plans are currently under active consideration:

- a retail sales tax
- a "flat" tax
- the Unlimited Savings Allowance (USA) tax
- a value-added tax

All four systems are conceived of as replacements for the federal income tax, both corporate and individual. In addition, the USA tax integrates the social security taxes through a system of credits.

As far as I know, no actual legislative proposal for a federal sales tax has yet been offered, but Representative

Bill Archer, chairman of the Ways and Means Committee of the House of Representatives, and Senator Richard Lugar have been notable supporters. A number of value-added tax proposals have been made, including a highly detailed plan introduced by Representative Samuel Gibbons. Representative Richard Armey is a particularly well-known advocate of a flat tax, although several others have advanced similar proposals. All of these are modeled on the flat tax developed by Robert Hall and Alvin Rabushka (1983, 1995), which I take as representative of the breed. Senators Pete Domenici and Sam Nunn developed the USA tax and introduced it in April 1995.[1]

All four approaches would bring about a shift of the U.S. tax system to a consumption base. In terms of implementation, the four have certain features in common. The first approach, a retail sales tax, is a proportional tax paid by businesses. The second and third, the flat tax and the USA tax, both consist of integrated systems. Each uses a proportional tax paid by businesses, more or less similar to a value-added tax, and a personal-level tax, along the lines of the existing individual income tax. In the case of the flat tax, the individual tax is imposed only on a person's compensation, such as wages and salary, which is deducted from the base of the business tax. The individual-level tax in the USA system is an example of what has come to be called a "consumed income" tax. That is to say, it is based on something like the present taxable income with a deduction for net saving (and inclusion of net dissaving). In the USA system, there is no deduction from the business tax base for payments to individuals (although there is a coordinated set of credits for payroll taxes).

My purpose here is not to provide a detailed description of any of these reforms. Instead, I use *uniform* (single-rate) income and consumption taxes,

- to show that the two approaches are, in principle,

much more similar than is generally understood
• to point out how it has proved difficult, in practice, to implement an income tax that treats investment uniformly and that is not affected by inflation
• to explain how the consumption approach is naturally inflation proof and naturally treats different kinds of investment uniformly
• to indicate the somewhat subtle ways in which shifting from an income to a consumption base may impose a one-time tax on "old savings" or "old capital"
• to indicate the trade-offs that must be confronted in dealing with this phenomenon
• to show how price-level changes that may or may not accompany a transition affect the distribution of gains and losses
• to sketch out how a transition might affect interest rates and asset prices (including owner-occupied housing)
• to explore the case in equity for protecting the tax-free recovery of old savings
• to emphasize the incentive problems that arise if savers and investors anticipate a change in the tax rate in a consumption-based system (A transition from zero to some positive rate upon introduction is a particularly important instance.)

By now, a considerable body of literature addresses the effects of time-varying tax policy, including transitions of the sort considered here. These analyses are complementary to my undertaking, which attempts both less, in raising but leaving open the answers to questions about the quantitative effects of policy changes, and more, in addressing aspects of transition on which the models to date are largely silent. For excellent examples of the technically more detailed models, see Auerbach and Kotlikoff (1983, 1987), Howitt and Sinn (1989), Keuschnigg (1991), and, especially, Sarkar and Zodrow (1993).

The study is organized as follows: In chapter 2, I explain how uniform consumption and income taxes can be implemented at the level of the business firm and develop the key differences between the two approaches. Chapter 3 describes the main transition issues, and chapter 4 addresses possible ways of dealing with them. In chapter 5, I touch on some of the arguments that go to the merits of seeking to moderate transition effects. Chapter 6 contains brief concluding remarks.

2

Key Concepts in Consumption and Income Taxation

As I have suggested, all four reform models bring about a switch to a consumption base. Just why this is so will be made clear by consideration of how one might administer either an income- or a consumption-based tax in the form of a tax paid by businesses.

Many people are familiar with the idea that a consumption tax can be administered in this way. Indeed, a retail-sales or value-added tax is often *identified* with "consumption tax." The idea that an income tax could be administered in much the same way is less familiar. It becomes obvious, however, if we start with a description of what is called in the jargon of the tax trade a *subtraction-method value-added tax of the consumption type*. The subtraction method is not the approach usually employed in value-added taxes, but it is the approach generally advocated in the United States. More important for my purpose here, it has a clear connection with the familiar income tax paid by businesses.

A Value-added Tax of the Consumption Type

The building block of a value-added tax, regardless of the method used, is the business firm subject to tax. Policy makers have quite a bit of scope in deciding just what is a "business firm" for this purpose. But I take for granted that no distinction is made between businesses according to legal form. In particular, there would normally be no difference between the treatment of corporations and other businesses, such as partnerships or proprietorships. So *business firm* is not the same thing as *corporation*, and *business tax* should not be identified with *corporation tax*.

Under a "subtraction method" of implementing a value-added tax, the tax base of a business consists of the difference between the payments it receives for sales of goods and services of any kind (including sales of assets, such as a building) and the purchases of goods and services from other firms. This total is then taxed at some predetermined fixed rate. That is it. In the ordinary case, financial transactions—such as borrowing and lending, issue and repurchase of stock, payments and receipts of dividends, and the like—do not enter the calculation of the taxable base.[2]

Because what is sold by one business to another results in an increase in the tax base of the selling firm and a deduction *at the same time and in exactly the same amount* by the purchasing firm, and since both are subject to tax at the same rate, transactions between businesses give rise to no *net* tax liability to the government.[3] The only circumstance under which a net tax liability is created is when there is a sale by a business to "the public," or more precisely, to a person or organization that is not a business firm subject to tax. At that point there is no deduction taken to offset the tax paid by the seller.

The aggregate business tax base is thus the sum of all sales by business to nonbusiness, which is a measure of aggregate consumption, one reason this is aptly called a consumption tax. (Another reason for calling it a consumption tax is the way saving and investment are treated, a matter I address later.)

How Does the Value-added Tax Relate to Other Reforms?

Retail Sales Tax. The subtraction-method value-added tax of the consumption type can be helpfully related to a variety of apparently different tax regimes. For example, because of this netting of the taxes on interbusiness transactions, a consumption-based subtraction-method value-added tax would result in the same revenue flow to the government as a tax on business-to-nonbusiness sales. In other words, a consumption-based subtraction-method value-added tax is fundamentally the same *economically* as a retail sales tax, even though it may look different and even though the two might be administered differently.[4]

Invoice-and-Credit Value-added Taxes. There is also a simple equivalence between a subtraction-method value-added tax and the invoice-and-credit form of value-added tax typically employed in other countries. European tax systems, for example, use the invoice-and-credit type of value-added tax. Under this method of taxation, the selling firm pays a tax on all sales, with no deductions, but claims a credit for taxes paid by the seller on purchases from other firms. The amount of the credit is the amount shown in the invoice from the selling firm, hence the name. If the tax rate of both businesses is the same, the credit obtained by the buying firm exactly equals the value of the deduction that would be claimed under the subtraction method. Thus, under both methods, a business-to-business sale results in a simultaneous, equal tax liability for the seller and tax credit for the buyer. No tax is paid to the government until the product or service is sold to a buyer who is not a taxable firm. This type of tax results in the same flow of revenues to the government as the subtraction-method value-added tax, or a retail sales tax for that matter, with the proviso that the same goods and services are subject to tax at the same rate.

Flat Tax. As has been mentioned, the flat tax consists of a coordinated pair of taxes, one levied on businesses, the other on individuals. The business tax component of the flat tax is a subtraction-method value-added tax of the consumption type with an important additional deduction for the business firm: payments to workers.[5] In turn, workers pay tax only on what they are paid by employers. The key insight is that if the tax on what workers receive is at the same rate as applies to employers, the net effect is the same as though there had been no deduction of the payments by the employer and no tax paid by the worker. In other words, the system would produce the same result as a subtraction-method value-added tax.

Under the flat tax, the rate of tax is the same for workers and employers. But for workers, the flat tax applies that rate only to the excess over an exempt amount that depends on the worker's family size. So the flat tax can be understood as (a) a subtraction-method consumption value-added tax, coupled with (b) a scheme based on workers' earnings designed to make the system progressive.

USA Tax. The USA tax also consists of a coordinated pair of taxes, one levied on businesses, the other on individuals. The business tax component of the USA tax is a subtraction-method value-added tax of the consumption type. To a first approximation (I neglect many fine points), the individual component of the USA tax can be understood as levied on a family's total consumption. The way it works is that the individual or married couple is taxed on all receipts of any kind, including receipts that result from sale of assets, with a deduction for any saved amounts, that is, for amounts used to acquire assets. The net amount, receipts not devoted to savings, must be used either for the purchase of consumption or for the payment of taxes. Under the individual component of the USA, the family is taxed on this measure of consumption according to graduated rates, just as in the existing individual income tax.[6]

What Kind of Beast Is a Consumption-Type VAT?

A Stage of Production Tax? A value-added tax is sometimes described as a tax levied at each successive stage of production. As applied to a uniform tax, this description is somewhat misleading because a sale at any intermediate stage in the production process that is subject to tax gives rise to an immediate offsetting deduction from a firm's tax base at the next stage of production. So no net tax is paid until the final stage of production, when the product is sold to the public.

A Transaction Tax? Sales and invoice-and-credit type value-added taxes are said to be transaction taxes. Some people draw a contrast between these types of taxes and income or subtraction-method value-added taxes, believing that the former are accounted for on a transaction-by-transaction basis, while the latter are aggregated on the company's books. In some contexts (such as regulatory accounting), the difference is of some significance, but it is a matter of legal form rather than economic substance. To figure out a company's income (and audit its tax accounts), we must add up individual amounts received (or payable) and subtract individual payments made (or payable). Under either a "book income" or "transaction tax" regime, it is necessary to keep track of and monitor individual transactions.

Under either regime, there is an enforcement advantage if the amount deducted from the tax base of (or amount of credit claimed by) one business should be matched exactly by an amount included in the tax base of (or amount of tax paid by) another. This will hold for consumption-type systems using either the subtraction or invoice-and-credit approaches. Under an income tax, however, this exact symmetry breaks down, because some of the deductions of the business buying capital equipment are spread over time in forms such as depreciation allowances.[7]

A Tax on Profits? Some assert that a value-added tax is the same as a tax on all the payments to factors of production—wages, salaries, and profits. This depends on how terms are defined.

As defined by accountants (economists sometimes use a different definition), *profit* includes the "normal" return entrepreneurs receive for waiting and taking risks plus any deviation, positive *or* negative, that results from the varying but statistically unpredictable fortunes of the firm. The return for risk taking, both its normal and its unpredictable component, is taxed identically under both an income tax and a consumption-type value-added tax. By contrast, because of differences in how a business firm's capital purchases are treated, the normal return for waiting is subjected to tax in an income tax but not in a consumption-based value-added tax.

The point is worth emphasizing. Like an income tax, a consumption-based value-added tax subjects to tax much of what is ordinarily understood as profit. If, for instance, a business discovers oil on its property, all the payoff is subject to tax. So is the reward for an innovation, such as the development of a successful software product, or the return on intangible property such as a trademark established through a successful advertising campaign. With a consumption-based value-added tax, the general public becomes a proportional shareholder in all enterprises.[8] If profits exceed the normal rate of return (risk adjusted), the general public shares in the good fortune. If they fall short, the general public, having "invested" via the deduction for investment outlays, shares in the shortfall.

Investments and Capital Income. With the value-added tax, business outlays for investment purposes—additions to inventory, to the stock of buildings, or to fixed equipment, for example—are deducted immediately. A successful investment will generate future tax liabilities that outweigh losses in revenues to the government due to current deductions. For a marginal investment, the cash flows consisting of the combination of the current tax saving and the anticipated future taxes due on the payoff to the investment will have a value of zero in the capital market. (More conventionally, if less precisely put, the expected net present discounted value of the combination is zero.) In this sense, a consumption-based value-added tax exempts income from capital. For what economists call an "extramarginal" investment—an investment opportunity that will beat the market—the tax is positive. (More precisely, the anticipated distribution of cash flows to the government will have a positive value in the capital market.)

In contrast, under an income-based tax, the deduction of the investment outlay is postponed. Conceptually, it is recovered as the value of the asset is depleted. This timing difference means that the profile of cash flow to the government associated with an investment that is a barely breakeven proposition will have a *positive* market value.

What is exempt from tax in a consumption-type tax system can be expressed in a variety of ways. One way is as the yield on a riskless investment, typically taken to be the Treasury bill rate. A consumption-based value-added tax allows investors to receive the Treasury bill rate on riskless investments, free of tax. A riskless rate of re-

turn in excess of this rate is taxed. A riskless rate of return below the market rate is compensated, in effect,
through reduced tax. In contrast, under a true income tax,
returns in excess of *zero* are taxed. To put this in quantitative perspective, the real riskless rate of return available to a tax-exempt investor has historically been below
1 percent per year.[9]

Is Risk Taking Taxed? The treatment of the reward to
bearing risk requires some analysis. Most assets do not
have a risk-free return. Even Treasury bills suffer from
the risk of unpredictable inflation. The average real rate
of return available to a tax-exempt investor in the stock
market has historically been about 9 percent per year.[10]
This higher average return is bought at the price of substantial risk. Can one also say that under a consumption-
type tax, the investor obtains the reward to risk taking
free of tax?

The answer is a qualified yes, but this is also the
answer to the same question with regard to an income
tax. This point is, I think, not widely understood probably
because we are accustomed to seeing risk and waiting in-
tertwined.[11] Under a uniform proportional income tax, a
pure bet that does not involve time is shared with the tax
collector on fair terms, through the allowance for losses.[12]
If there is a risk premium, a uniform tax will have positive expected revenue, but it will not impose a burden on
the investor. The positive expected revenue is the risk
premium collected by the government for assuming part
of the risk, via the tax system.

The same result is obtained under a consumption-
type tax, except that the cash flow to the government may
not be simultaneous with the outcome of risk taking, so
that the argument needs to take into account discounting
for differences in timing. Essentially, an income tax and a
consumption tax treat risk the same. Essentially, under

both systems, any positive expected revenue is the market-determined reward for the risk that the government takes and is not a burden to the taxed investor.

Is a Value-added Tax a Wage Tax? It is often said that a value-added tax of the consumption type is equivalent to a tax on wages or a tax on labor income. Again, whether this is so depends on one's definition of the terms *wages* or *labor income*. The payoff to the oil gusher or the successful advertising campaign or the development of Microsoft DOS might not be regarded as wages or labor income in ordinary parlance. But these are subject to a value-added tax of the consumption type.

As the discussion above of the effective taxation of risk bearing suggests, in either case the tax may or may not represent a burden. We may think of the activity of an individual entrepreneur or firm as one of selection from "ideas" that arise, perhaps randomly or perhaps as a result of investment of funds and effort. The unprofitable ideas are rejected. Those that are accepted are believed to be, at least, breakeven propositions in the sense that the associated distribution of cash flows will have a market value at least zero.

Both consumption- and income-tax systems will place a burden on profitable ideas. The resulting incentive effects will depend on the details of the process by which ideas are generated.[13] To the extent that oil gushers and the like represent just the upside of investments that were expected to produce the risk-adjusted market rate of return, the positive revenue in a consumption-type system is just the market-determined reward to the to the government (that is, other taxpayers) for taking on risk. Under a true income tax there is, in any case, a burden put on postponement of consumption, as reflected in the risk-free real interest rate; in the same sense, a disinvestment project is subsidized.

Is Owner-occupied Housing Taxed? The income tax in the United States exempts the yield from investment in household capital, by which I mean durables such as automobiles, boats, washing machines, electronic equipment, and the like. Quantitatively, the most important example is owner-occupied housing (including second homes). To capture such capital in an income tax would involve treating the household as in the business of selling to itself the services of these investments. Because the income tax does not attempt to do this, it puts such forms of investment at an advantage, relative to ordinary business capital.

One of the features of consumption-based taxes that makes them appeal to economists is that they could, in a simple way, tax household capital on an even plane with business capital. (See, for example, Jorgenson 1995.) This result would obtain not by setting up the household as a business under a value-added tax of the subtraction type. Rather, these implicit businesses are left out of the set of firms subject to tax. The advantage for these implicit firms is that they are not subject to tax on their implicit sales (for example, the sale of housing services by owner-occupiers to themselves). The disadvantage is that they are not eligible to deduct (in the case of the invoice-and-credit approach, obtain credit for the taxes paid on) their purchases. With a taxable business, the general public shares in the investment and payoffs in proportion to the tax rate. In making investment decisions, the taxable firm considers its share. For a tax-exempt household "business," the general public does not share in the investment or the return. The investment decision is based on the full cost and the full return. The breakeven requirement will be the same for a taxable and tax-exempt business.

If the sale of housing is treated like all other sales under a subtraction-method value-added tax, it will remove the tax advantage that owner-occupied housing enjoys under the income tax.[14] A question of some interest is what this change will imply for the value of existing houses. I take up this question below.

A Value-added Tax Could Be an Income Tax

It may not be well known that a value-added tax could be used to implement an income tax. To do so requires, essentially, using conventional income accounting for the firm's income, instead of the cash-flow accounting used in the consumption-type tax, although to do it "right" would require making systematic corrections for inflation.[15] An income statement should report the change in the firm's net worth during the year. When a firm acquires a unit of capital equipment, it exchanges one asset (money in the bank) for another (the purchased equipment). If the investment is wise and expected in the capital market, the value of the firm does not change. That is the logic behind the fact that accountants "capitalize" such outlays for purposes of income accounting, which means they are not deducted currently. Over time, however, equipment typically declines in value. This decline must be accounted for in the income statement, even though it does not correspond to current cash flow. That is why accountants take depreciation charges in their measure of current income.

Similarly, when goods are acquired to augment inventory, the cash outlay for purchases does not result in a change in the business's net worth. It is added to the stock of inventory assets. The accountants register the cost of producing or acquiring inventory later, in the form of a deduction for the cost of goods sold. Associating past outlays for inventory with current receivables is one of many problems related to pinning down accounting concepts for income purposes that do not arise in the cash-flow accounting system appropriate for a consumption-based tax system.

The essential difference between income accounting and consumption-based accounting is timing. A tax on a firm's income would be based on the difference between amounts received from sales and a measure of the firm's costs, including recovery of past outlays for equipment, inventories, and such. When a business-to-business sale occurs, the purchasing firm deducts the amount paid from its income calculation. Generally, that deduction is less than the invoiced price because the purchaser must capitalize some of the outlay, to be recovered in future income calculations.

There is a sense in which a true income tax, by contrast with a subtraction-method value-added tax, would effect a tax at each stage of production. This point is most easily understood by assuming that each stage of production is carried out by a different firm.[16] The aggregate amount subject to tax would equal the difference between the value of the goods and services sold and the *discounted value* of the future deductions by purchasing firms in the form of depreciation allowances and other forms of cost recovery. The aggregate of the taxable incomes of all the firms would equal the sum of the sales to the public and the net increase in the stock of capitalized past outlays in the hands of the firms. As described above, the former is aggregate consumption, and the latter (which could be negative) is a measure of the increase in aggregate net worth, or saving.[17] (Theoretically, the tax calculation for a vertically integrated company that combines several stages of production should lead to the same result.)

This exercise highlights four important aspects of consumption and income as tax bases:

•First, it emphasizes the role of timing. The distinction between an income and a consumption tax is essentially a matter of timing—the time value of money. (In both systems the costs of production are recovered, but costs are recovered earlier under a consumption tax.)

• Second, it demonstrates that an indirect tax can be employed to implement a uniform income tax, just as one is accustomed to thinking one can use such a system to impose a uniform consumption tax.[18]

• Third, it highlights important differences in accounting. Income accounting is more difficult than cash-flow accounting. That difficulty is responsible for much of the complexity in the current income tax system. (This is a major theme of Bradford 1986.)

• Fourth, it explains why, at any given time under an income tax a company has a stock of past outlays that may be thought of as an accumulation of tax-prepaid claims on future consumption. These claims, represented by "basis" in the company's assets, belong to the company's owners. This assumes great significance in any transition from an income- to a consumption-based tax system.

Deductions for Wages and Interest and the VAT

With the subtraction-method value-added tax regime, little would change if companies were permitted to deduct payments to employees, provided those payments were subject to tax, at the same rate. (That is, the tax saving to the employer would exactly equal the extra payments to employees necessary to leave them in the same place after tax.) The government would receive the same cash flow, and the economic effects should be identical. More generally, payments to workers might be subject to tax at a different rate, or on a graduated schedule, without changing the essential economics. As we have noted, if the schedule were to consist of an exempt amount plus a single rate for amounts above the exempt amount (the same single rate applied to firms), the result would be what we have identified as a flat tax.

The same idea extends to interest payments in a

value-added tax regime. Little of economic substance would change if companies were allowed to deduct interest paid to creditors, as well as payments to employees if the tax rate for these income recipients was the same as the business-level tax. Apart from graduated rates, this is a rough approximation of how the combination of corporate and individual income taxes currently operates. If the same tax rate applies to the deduction by the firm and inclusion in taxable income of bondholders, the result should be the same as a value-added tax with no such deductions.[19]

The concept of deducting interest and taxing it at the bondholder level is introduced here because the commitment to make interest payments according to a fixed contract creates an important problem of transition to a regime with no interest deduction. Bondholders can be expected to require compensation for assuming tax obligations; thus the stated interest rate will be different when interest can be deducted from when it is not. When no tax is incurred at the bondholder level, the bondholder receives an after-tax interest rate; with the other treatment of interest, the stated rate will be the before-tax rate.

3

Transition Issues

We often describe the distribution of tax burdens in terms of the progressivity of a continuing system—the relative tax burdens imposed on people at different levels of income. But a major change in the tax system causes one-time gains and losses that may be only loosely related to the progressivity of the system either before or after the change. Introduction of a value-added tax of the consumption type provides an excellent and highly relevant instance of this point.

Imagine that we have been operating under a proportional value-added tax of the income type and a decision is made to switch to a consumption-type tax (basically by substituting expensing of investment outlays for depreciation allowances over time). Under both these tax regimes, broadly speaking, burdens are spread proportionally to income levels. In the course of a *switch* from one to the other, however, there may be one-time burdens that fall much more heavily on owners of business capital, on those who have saved in the past, and on older citizens than on others. Indeed, the "others" may be significant gainers. One may like or not like this result. Depending on what one wants to emphasize, one may say the transition effect is highly progressive or very unfair to those who have accumulated savings in the past. But it is unlikely the effect will bear any systematic relationship to the usual standards by which we judge tax distributions.

Whether such effects will be significant will depend on the allowance made in the rules for transition to the new system. By examining the particularly simple case of uniform income and consumption taxes, we can highlight the essential problems. The existing system is approximated by a value-added tax of the *income* type and the reforms as a switch to a value-added tax of the *consumption* type. This switch can be analyzed by a two-step procedure. First, consider the effect of introducing the value-added tax of the *consumption* type, and then consider the offsetting effect of eliminating the tax of the *income* type. To start with, I focus on the cases where there is only a business tax, with no deduction of wages or interest and no taxation at the individual level.

One-Time Asset Tax

One concrete example captures the essence of the problem. It is the case of a retail store, whose owners have purchased, on the day before the value-added tax is introduced, a stock of canned goods for $10,000. They sell the goods the day after the value-added tax is introduced, say at a rate of 20 percent. In calculating the business's value-added tax liability, the proceeds from the sale of the canned goods are on the inclusion side of the ledger. In the normal course of events, there would have been a deduction in the past for the purchase of those goods. But at the moment of introduction of the new tax, the purchase of the goods is already a thing of the past. Applying the new rules, there is a tax of $2,000 on the sale of the canned goods from inventory but no offsetting deduction. Barring special rules, the effect of introducing the new system is to impose a one-time tax, at the value-added tax rate, on the stock of inventory at the time of transition.

This story, writ large, captures the essence of the way introducing a consumption-type tax, with no special transition rules, would impose a one-time tax on the stock of wealth in the economy, so-called old capital or old savings. In the example, the extra tax on the stock of inventory was imposed immediately, because the goods were sold to the public on day one of the new system. In actuality, the tax payments that give effect to the one-time tax would take place over time, for example, over the lifetime of a piece of fixed equipment. But the discounted present value of the extra tax imposed is the same as if the assets were sold immediately to the public (provided the tax rate is constant). So the effect is the same, even though the payments are spread out in time.

Most people, of course, do not own retail stores. Instead, their ownership interest in businesses is indirect, through stock in corporations. Even the ownership of stock may be indirect. It may, for example, be through a claim on a defined-contribution pension plan that in turn owns stock. But the one-time tax effect will carry through to these indirect owners. Imposing a value-added tax of the consumption type would be predicted to cause a fall in the market value of stock commensurate with the extra one-time tax liability. I use the term *commensurate* here because one critical aspect of the adjustment to the new system that I have not yet discussed will have a large effect on the transition incidence. That is the impact of the policy change on the general level of prices.

Price Level Changes. Most people assume that companies will "pass forward" a newly introduced value-added tax in the form of higher prices. It is important to recognize that whether or not this occurs (1) is not a matter that is settled by well-developed theory and (2) does not affect the one-time wealth tax due to introducing the new tax, although it may affect the way the burden of that tax is distributed. In a competitive economy, a value-added tax of the consumption type must be extracted from the difference between the value of goods sold by companies and what they pay to noncompany suppliers, which we may here take to be workers. That much is clear. Whether, however, a newly introduced tax leads to an increase in the prices of things sold or a decrease in the wages of workers is not well determined. It will depend on the institutions of wage and price setting and on monetary policy. It is commonly believed, however, that introducing a value-added tax of the consumption type will bring with it a monetary policy adjustment that results in a one-time increase in the price level (not a change in the *rate* of inflation) and no change in payments to workers in *nominal* terms (so that, before taking into account any offsetting reduction in income taxation, nominal wages are unchanged but *real* wages of workers decline by the amount of the tax). By contrast, it is generally thought that introducing a tax levied on the earnings of workers will lead to a decrease in their take-home pay and no change in the prices charged by companies. The real result for workers is the same.

If there *is* a change in the price level and if this change in price level has not been anticipated and therefore built into transactions expressed in dollar terms (for example, through an adjustment in interest rates), then introducing the value-added tax of the consumption type will bring about a redistribution of wealth from lenders to borrowers, through a decline of the real value of the dollar.

Leverage and the Wealth Tax Effect. That the matter is of some importance, and that policy makers might want to encourage such an "accommodating" monetary policy, is suggested by considering the situation of the business owners who have financed the acquisition of business assets by issuing debt with fixed nominal terms. In my example, suppose the store's owners have borrowed the $10,000 to buy the inventory of canned goods, expecting to sell the goods the next day for a little more than $10,000 and repay the loan. (Interest on the loan is not important in this very short-term transaction.) If, in the meantime, the value-added tax has been introduced *and* there is no change in the price level, the owners of the inventory will suffer a loss equal to $2,000—the tax rate times $10,000. They will suffer this loss *even though they have no net wealth at all*, since their assets in the form of inventory are just balanced by their liabilities in the form of the loan. The one in this picture who does have some wealth, the lender who holds the $10,000 note, will experience no loss from the new tax. He or she will still be able to take the proceeds of the loan repayment and buy the same goods and services as if there were no new tax.

By contrast, if the price level increases by the amount of the tax, the owners of the inventory will suffer no loss; they will have $10,000 left after tax with which to repay the loan. Instead, the transition loss will be borne by the lender, via the erosion of the purchasing power of the $10,000.[20]

Translating this story to the stock market, if the transition brings with it an unexpected one-time increase in the price level, the transition loss, measured in real purchasing power, will be spread evenly across the debt and equity holders. Equities would keep their market value but lose in real value a proportion equal to the tax rate, and the same would be true of nominally denominated assets and liabilities. At the other polar case of no adjustment in the price level (actually, *polar case* is a somewhat misleading term here; anything could happen), nominally denominated assets and liabilities would keep their real value and the entire loss, of the tax rate times the sum of equity *and* debt value, would be borne by equity holders. As in the case of the store owner who paid for the inventory with borrowed money, there is a leveraged effect on the equity holders that could be substantial.[21]

A Tax on the Elderly? An important question is who are the owners of assets who would bear the cost of transition to a consumption-type tax (barring special provisions to mitigate the effect)? As has just been emphasized, the impact of the transition will depend both on the extent to which it is accompanied by price-level changes *and* on the composition of people's portfolios (especially the division between nominal and real assets and liabilities). It is generally assumed that the effect will be roughly proportional to wealth (that is, either wealth owners have similar portfolios or there is an unanticipated price-level adjustment). Apart from knowing that the distribution of wealth ownership is highly skewed, with a large fraction of wealth owned by a relatively small fraction of the population, we also know that, owing to life-cycle factors in the process of accumulation, wealth is also correlated with age. This means that the policy regarding transition to a consumption-type tax should be thought about in the framework of intergenerational distribution.

Many commentators (in particular, Kotlikoff 1992 and Auerbach, Gokhale, and Kotlikoff 1993) have noted the tendency of fiscal policy in the United States over the past thirty years to shift the net burden of financing the government away from older and toward younger and future generations. To the extent that this tendency describes fundamental political factors, it would suggest we should expect to see any transition to a consumption-type tax accompanied by rules that would protect the interests of older generations. To the extent that there is a movement toward readjusting the fiscal balance (arguably, the proper economic interpretation of "deficit-reduction"), we might expect to see a transition to a consumption-type tax taken as an opportunity to lighten the projected burdens of young and future generations.

The Effect on the Analysis of Taxing Wages at the Level of the Worker. If we modify the example to permit companies a deduction for wages, there will be a change in the locus of tax payments—the bulk of tax collections will be from workers, rather than businesses—but, from a formal point of view, none of the issues discussed above will be affected. I use the word *formal* advisedly, since it is commonly believed that workers are likely to resist changes in their before-tax wages. If before-tax wages are fixed and wages are not allowed as a deduction, then the price level must increase to accommodate the tax.

If wages are allowed as a deduction (and taxed at the worker level), holding constant the level of wages before tax means a reduction in wages after tax. In that case, there would be no adjustment in the price level necessary to establish equilibrium in the relationship between prices and wages.

Effects from Eliminating an Income Tax

Our idealized tax reform involves introduction of a consumption-type tax and elimination of an income-type tax, represented in the present analysis by a value-added tax of the income type. Under a value-added tax of the income type, the yield on business investment is taxed, at the value-added tax rate, at the business level. In the pure case, there is no tax at the individual level. Interest (along with other forms of reward to owners of capital) is "pre-taxed" at the company level.[22] In an equilibrium with a value-added tax of the income type, the interest rate on financial assets would equal the *after-tax* rate of return on investment. This is in contrast to the result when interest is deducted by business borrowers and taxed in the hands of the individual. In that case, the interest rate tends to equality with the before-tax rate of return on business investment.

Under a value-added tax of the consumption type, changes in the tax rate (for example, from zero to a positive rate at the time of introduction of the tax) produce changes in the value of a company along the lines just discussed. By contrast, under an income-type tax, with proper accounting rules, changes in the rate of tax do not produce changes in the market value of assets. (The qualification, "with proper accounting rules," is important. Technically, what is required is that the basis of assets be equal to their market value. With accelerated depreciation, for example, basis will be less than market value. In that case, a decline in the income tax rate produces an increase in a company's value, because of the reduction in the tax liability that will come due when the difference between the asset's basis and its market value is realized in future transactions.)

Consequently, the transition issues raised by a switch from a pure value-added tax of the income type to a pure value-added tax of the consumption type are the same as those involved in introducing value-added tax from a situation with no tax.

Effect of a Regime Shift on Interest and Assets

Thus far I have focused on transition effects apart from effects on relative prices. Among the most important of the latter are the interest rate and its correlative, asset prices. Changes of policy of the magnitude under consideration here might be expected to produce significant changes in interest rates and asset prices. Unfortunately, asset price effects are hard to predict; yet they may constitute an important part of the transition story. Since my objective is to lay out issues, not necessarily to resolve them, I sketch out here the implications of what might be taken to be the polar possibilities.

The effect of the policy shift on asset prices will depend on two major dimensions of the economy's response. One dimension is, in economists' jargon, the relative demand and supply elasticities of capital. At one extreme of this spectrum is the "infinite elasticity of demand for capital" assumption that the opportunities to invest at the going rate of return are unlimited within the relevant range. This might be a good description of the situation of a small country well connected to world capital markets. The before-tax rate of interest is unaffected by policy changes in the small country. At the other extreme of this spectrum is the "infinite elasticity of supply of capital" assumption that the amount of wealth people are willing to hold at the going rate of return to savers is unlimited within the relevant range. This assumption can be justified on the basis of very long life-cycle or dynastic purposes of saving (Summers 1981). Under this assumption, a country's tax policy has no effect on the after-tax rate of return received by savers, since they will spend down their wealth if the after-tax rate of return is lower and accumulate if the after-tax rate of return is higher.

The second dimension of response that is important in determining the effect of the reform is the cost of adjustment. To illustrate, suppose we introduced a tax credit for new investment in equipment. For a company with a given investment opportunity, this would appear to offer extra profit. But if other companies can rush to take advantage of the same opportunity, the extra profit will be dissipated in lower prices of the extra output or higher prices of the equipment in question. Where the balance will be struck will depend on the extent to which the incumbent company has a cost advantage in undertaking the new investment.

The higher costs of other companies are what is re-

ferred to as the cost of adjustment. And the effect of the
rules that make investment more attractive at given interest rates will be influenced by the extent to which owners of existing capital have a temporary advantage over
potential competitors for investment opportunities when
interest rates fall. When the temporary advantage is large,
the incumbents, those who already own business assets,
can earn supernormal profits during an adjustment period during which new assets are constructed. At the other
extreme of this dimension of response, if new assets can
be put in place instantaneously, with no extra cost, the
price of existing assets will equal their replacement cost,
regardless of interest rate changes. So the new rules will
have no effect on the prices of reproducible assets. If, as is
certainly the case to some degree, expanding the capital
stock quickly brings with it extra costs, owners of existing
assets will reap a capital gain on a change that leads to a
higher level of the capital stock.

The opposite effect applies to owners of assets for
which adjustment requires a fall in the stock. This might
be the case for assets that are favored by the existing tax
law. Under a true, uniform income tax, all assets are
treated alike. We would then expect a shift to a new regime to call for expansion or contraction of all asset stocks.
But under the actual income tax, some assets are more
lightly taxed than others, and a shift to a uniform consumption-type tax that might call forth an expansion of
regular business investment might involve contraction in
the stocks of formerly tax-favored assets. Adjustment cost
in this case refers to the time required to work off an excess in the supply of an asset type, relative to that justified by the costs of reproduction. The practical case of such
an asset of most importance is owner-occupied housing,
which I discuss further below.[23]

In view of the influence of such assumptions on the
results, the analysis here can indicate only the nature of

transition problems. The magnitudes and even the directions of change cannot be inferred from general principles.

Interest Rates. If adjustment costs were zero, eliminating a uniform business tax on accretion income would not change business asset prices, except insofar as they reflected any transition wealth tax. The policy change could, however, lead to a change in the rate of interest received by savers. At the one pole is an unchanged rate of return on investment before tax. Since the tax being eliminated was paid at the business level, competition would drive up the rate of interest by the amount of the former tax. The interest rate net of tax would therefore rise by the amount of the former income tax rate, providing wealth owners with a higher yield. At the other pole is an unchanged rate of interest net of tax, the case of "infinitely elastic" supply of capital. In this case the market rate of interest would be unchanged, but expansion of the capital stock would result in driving down the rate of return on investment by the amount of the former tax. Wealth holders would see no change in the yield on their holdings.

If interest were taxed at the level of the recipient, rather than at the level of the paying firm, the outcomes would be the same, but since the market rate of interest would then be a before-tax rate, the description would need to be revised accordingly.

Concentrating on the case of no change in the before-tax yield on investment, we see that the higher rate of return works to compensate wealth holders for the loss imposed on transition to the consumption-type tax. Whether a particular wealth holder gains or loses depends critically on the planned timing of consumption. For people who are planning to draw down their wealth in the near future, even a very large increase in the rate of return will not compensate for the one-time loss. For people who are planning to defer consumption for a long time, the one-time wealth loss will be more than made up by the increased yield.[24]

The analysis of these polar cases establishes several points:

•In general, imposition of a consumption-type tax will cause a one-time loss to owners of certain assets. The loss will be spread over all wealth owners to the extent the transition is accompanied by an unanticipated increase in the price level.

•Substitution of a consumption-type tax for an income-type tax may bring with it a higher after-tax yield to holders of wealth.

•A higher yield is a compensating factor for a transition wealth loss, but the offset depends on the consumption plans of the holders. Those planning long postponement will gain. Those planning near-term consumption will lose. If there is no increase in the yield on wealth, there is no compensating offset to the loss of wealth on transition.

•There is thus a considerable range of outcomes possible, depending in particular on the response of the rate of return on saving to the change in policy and on the distribution of preferences in the wealth-holding population.

Empirical research will be required to draw more specific conclusions.

Owner-occupied Housing. The effect of reform on the value of owner-occupied housing is a matter of great political moment. Just as in the case of other assets, the effect of a transition to a consumption-based tax on owner-occupied housing has two elements. First is any tendency for the transition to effect a one-time tax on this form of real asset. The good news is that real assets in the hands of households, including consumer durables and inventories of goods, as well as houses for personal use, are not subject to the one-time tax. We may contrast the situation of a person in the business of building houses for sale, who would confront the wealth tax in transition, because the sale of a house in inventory would be subject to the consumption tax. That house would compete in the market with houses already owned by households and would therefore sell for the same price.

The second element is the case of adjustment costs. In connection with the discussion of business capital above, the case of no adjustment costs was highlighted. In that case, the stock of business capital is assumed to adjust so that all forms of investment have the same yield at the margin (the going interest rate). The corresponding assumption for owner-occupied housing would lead to the same result: the value of the stock of housing would not be affected by any change in the interest rate brought about by the shift in tax regime.[25]

To illustrate the effect of positive adjustment costs, suppose the stock of housing in the income tax era is adjusted to yield the after-tax risk-free interest rate of 1.5 percent when the market risk-free interest rate, before tax, is 2 percent. Owner-occupied housing will attract investment until its yield, which is exempt from tax, is 1.5 percent. The regime shift produces a decline in the market interest rate to, say, 1.75 percent as a result of an expansion of saving and capital accumulation. To get to a yield of 1.75 percent on the margin in housing investment requires a downward adjustment in the stock of housing. We might expect such a downward adjustment to take time, which is to say to involve adjustment costs. In this case, the regime shift would have a depressing effect on housing prices and result in losses to owners of housing capital.

Interest at the Individual Level

A simplified version of a shift to a consumption-type tax from something like the present tax system would involve a change from an income-type tax with a deduction at the level of the firm for interest payments and wage payments (and taxation, at the same rate, at the level of wage and interest recipients) to a consumption-type tax at the business level with no deduction for interest (or taxation of interest received) and possibly no deduction for wages (and in that case, no taxation of wages received). I have argued that the equilibrium results obtained should not depend on the level (payer or recipient) at which interest or wages are taxed. The alternative tax treatments will be reflected in compensating differences in the terms of the transactions between payers and recipients. There is, however, a potential transition problem posed by contracts entered into in one tax regime that are to be carried out in the other.

Starting with a system that taxes interest and wage payments at the level of the individual implies the existence of commitments, fixed for some period of time, that will incorporate the expectations of the parties about the tax treatment of the payments. Consider first the case in which the shift to a consumption-type tax is *not* accompanied by a change in the general price level. Then, during the period covered by the contractual commitment, the interest recipient or wage recipient under a contract made before the change will gain, and the payer will lose. The gains and losses will be simply the amount of the tax.

Alternatively, if there is a one-time price level change in connection with introduction of the consumption-type tax, the purchasing power of the recipient who no longer pays tax will be the same as before the change. The transition problem is thus linked to the price level determination.

It may be reasonable to single out interest commitments in this regard, as being fixed for a longer term than is likely in other contracts and, perhaps, as being less amenable to renegotiation. (In a sense, most employment contracts are in a continual process of renegotiation.) But the difference is one of degree.

4

Moderating Transition Effects

At the business level, two points at which special
transition rules would seem likely are basis in assets and liabilities and commitments to interest
with a presumption of deductibility established before the
shift in regimes. The more generous the allowances, the
less the potential loss from transition, at a cost in revenue that must be made up in a higher tax rate in the
new system.

Basis in Business Assets

For the simple case of substitution, overnight, of a uniform subtraction-method value-added tax of the consumption type for a uniform income tax, a "cold turkey" transition would effect a one-time tax on the holders of real assets, perhaps reallocated to the holders of wealth more
generally, through price-level effects.[26] To eliminate any
one-time tax on existing real assets would require allowing immediate deduction of the company's basis. As for
past investment, immediate deduction of the company's
basis would put previous investment on the income-tax
system up to the time of the switch and on the consumption-tax system from then on. We can describe allowing

such a deduction as a policy of fully protecting "old capital."[27]

It is often said that protecting old capital in this way would unacceptably increase the government's budget deficit. Dealing with the deficit consequences is, however, a matter of structuring the rules to achieve the desired cash flow. Thus, an economically equivalent policy to permitting immediate write-off of existing basis would be to permit write-off over a period of time, as long as desired, provided there were an allowance of interest earnings on as yet undeducted basis. The effect would be to provide taxpayers with the same discounted value of tax savings as immediate deduction, but the cash flow to the government would be very different.

The revenue effect of taxing or not taxing existing stocks of assets is, however, not a matter of detail. In their modeling of such transitions, for example, Auerbach and Kotlikoff (1987) conclude that a switch from an income tax to a consumption tax, while fully protecting old capital (a policy they refer to as a wage tax) might well generate an effective reduction in national welfare, whereas a switch that provided no protection to old savings would generate large gains in every case. These consequences stem from the lump-sum character of the one-time tax on wealth (in their analysis, they treat the change as unanticipated), which allows a lower tax rate and thereby enhances future efficiency.

Such particular conclusions are a function of the specifics of the modeling of the economy and the policies. (For example, Auerbach and Kotlikoff do not incorporate the smoothing of revenues that might be accomplished by delaying the recovery of basis along the lines discussed above.) The generic point is, however, unavoidable, and it is a centrally important element of policy choice. A one-time tax on old savings can generate a great deal of revenue, and if it is really unanticipated, it can do so with no efficiency cost at all, just the distributional consequences discussed above. I return below to both the efficiency and the distributional questions.

As an alternative to fully protecting old capital, permitting businesses to continue to take as deductions against the value-added tax of the consumption type the depreciation allowances to which they would have been entitled under the income tax might seem a reasonable policy. It would appear to fulfill the expectations of businesses that had made investments with certain assumptions about the tax treatment of the transactions. As the discussion thus far should make clear, however, this approach is not the same as fully protecting existing assets from the one-time tax that would result from a simple switch to consumption-tax rules. The pattern of incidence is also somewhat curious: owners of assets with short remaining lives would be closest to fully protected, while those owning assets with long remaining depreciable lives, such as recently constructed buildings, would come closest to incurring the full one-time tax. It is not clear such a pattern of incidence has anything to offer in terms of either efficiency or equity.

Preexisting Commitments to Pay Interest

As I have suggested, the commitment to pay interest would seem particularly prominent among the various preexisting commitments that might attract special transitional treatment. I have also suggested that adjustment for preexisting commitments will occur automatically if there is a one-time price level change. In the alternative case of no change in the price level, it would appear feasible in the framework of *uniform* systems to adopt a grandfathering approach. With regard to those commitments that predate the transition to the new system, retain the old tax rules. The deduction by one taxpayer and the inclusion by another taxpayer at the same rate of tax have no allocational significance, but if the applicable tax rate is the same in the income and the consumption-tax systems, both borrowers and lenders will be unaffected by the change in rules. This observation applies to deduction by mortgage borrowers of interest on preexisting contracts, just as it does to businesses.

The neat symmetry and simplicity of this transition rule would be considerably complicated by the presence of multiple rates of tax (for example, both taxable and tax-exempt entities) in the preexisting system or in the new system. In some way, preserving preexisting expectations with regard to interest payments and receipts may, however, provide a way to moderate a transition effect that has no obvious policy merit. (That effect is imposing an unexpected burden on borrowers and providing an unexpected windfall on lenders by virtue of the change in treatment of payments labeled interest.)

The issue of the treatment of prechange commitments to pay and receive interest needs to be distinguished from the issue of the effect of the change in the rate of interest as a relative price. If the after-tax interest rate increases as a consequence of the regime shift, net creditors will gain and net debtors will lose. This phenomenon is taken up in the next chapter.

5

Should Old Capital Be Taxed?

Thus far I have concentrated on the burden-shifting effects of a switch between a uniform income tax and a uniform consumption tax. There are two important incentive-related aspects of the transition.

Effects of Transition on Saving and Investing

First, as has been discussed, the one-time wealth tax potentially provides the revenue to permit a relatively low tax in the new system. Economists describe such a tax as "lump-sum" because there is no behavioral change by which a person can avoid its impact. (The classic textbook lump-sum tax is a poll tax.) The advantage of a lump-sum tax is that, since it cannot be avoided through behavioral changes, it does not distort economic choices. If it is true that the transition is in the nature of a lump-sum tax, it would provide revenue to reduce taxes that do distort behavior, such as taxes on earnings from work or saving. As demonstrated by Auerbach and Kotlikoff (1987 and especially 1983), the gains from lower tax rates could actually permit everyone, including those on whom the one-time wealth tax is imposed, to gain from the transition.[28]

One can, however, make too much of the supposed lump-sum character of a cold-turkey transition. To be a lump-sum tax, the tax on wealth must be unanticipated. Otherwise people will take steps to avoid the tax by consuming more rapidly, saving and investing less. This is the second important efficiency aspect of transition. An anticipated introduction of a consumption tax, or an anticipated *increase in its rate,* for which no compensating transition rule is provided, will discourage saving and investing and encourage current consumption. Assets held at the time of an increase in rate suffer a one-time percentage tax equal to the change in the consumption-tax rate. There is an incentive to convert assets to consumption before the rate change. An investment project will result in a deduction today at the lower rate, but its future payoff will be taxed at the higher rate. There is an incentive to postpone investment projects. It is easy to see that these incentive effects could be very strong.

Concern about incentive effects of this sort leads policy makers to establish an "effective date" on the day of first serious consideration of programs, such as an investment tax credit, designed to encourage investment. It is recognized that an anticipation that investment will be more favorably treated in the future than in the present will lead to a postponement, typically the very opposite of the desired effect.

There is, finally, the reputational effect of imposing a one-time tax on transition. If as a result, taxpayers are wary of future such "one-time" changes, their incentives for forward looking investment are no longer captured by whatever purport to be the current rules. Instead, investors will behave as though there were a tax, since they are at risk of a change in the rules and lack any assurance that transition impacts of such a change will be ameliorated through appropriate rules. This is the problem of time consistency.

Political Economy Arguments

There is a certain contradiction in the idea that imposition of a consumption-type tax is unexpected and therefore is effectively a lump-sum tax, with no disincentive consequences, whereas an increase in the *rate* of a consumption tax may be anticipated, discouraging investment. The logic is, "We'll only do this just this once." The *potential* that a government *may* introduce a consumption-type tax without compensating transition rules presumably has disincentive effects as soon as it is felt to be operative (as perhaps in the present time). In any case, once a consumption-type tax is in place, the consequences of anticipated changes need to be taken into account.

There are basically two directions to take toward dealing with this problem on a more systematic basis. The first is to design into the systems mechanisms that limit the variability in tax rates. An example would be enacting special majority rules for tax rate increases. Another example is the self-averaging feature of the cash flow tax described in the U.S. Treasury's *Blueprints for Basic Tax Reform* (U.S. Treasury 1977; also Bradford et al. 1984). In briefest sketch, the *Blueprints* cash-flow tax would operate wholly at the level of the individual (rather than the firm), producing a consumption-type base by allowing deduction of net deposits to "qualified accounts" and otherwise leaving interest and similar flows out of the tax base. The resulting base would be taxed at graduated rates. In such a system it would be in the individual taxpayer's interest to "self-average" to maintain a constant tax rate over time.[29] Self-averaging is generally thought of as a way to deal with variation in the individual's tax base, due to life cycle or other sources of changing economic circumstances. But self-averaging could also deal with anticipated changes in legislation, leading taxpayers to engineer a current tax increase for themselves in anticipation of an upward shift in the tax rate schedule to be brought about through legislation or a tax decrease in anticipation of a downward shift in the tax rate schedule. In the process, adverse incentive effects on investment would be eliminated.

The second approach is to establish a principle or mechanism to ensure that changes in rates will be accompanied by measures to reduce or eliminate the effective wealth levies, for example, by grandfathering provisions. (Another example of such a device is the common practice in the legislative process, when investment incentives are likely to be affected by rule changes, of announcing an effective date after which transactions will come under the new rules if enacted.) It seems easier to imagine grandfathering rules to protect taxpayers from having their wealth taken by a rate increase than ones that would extract the wealth gain from a tax rate cut. A practical instance of such a gain was effected by the Tax Reform Act of 1986, which resulted in substantial reductions in the taxes on pension benefits that had been deducted earlier at higher marginal rates.

There is thus an interaction between a general practice of protecting investors from the sort of wealth tax that we have been discussing and the degree to which tax rate changes need to be inhibited.

Equity Arguments

Early and Late Consumers. There are two main strands of equity arguments in connection with the transition to a consumption-type tax.[30] The first one focuses on the fact that, under a consumption-type tax, owners of wealth will obtain their normal yield free of further tax. This applies to wealth accumulated after the transition and is an aspect of the argument in favor of the consumption approach. But for those who accumulated their wealth before the transition, goes the argument, the new rules may effect an unexpected, if not undeserved, gain.

As discussed above, any one-time tax on wealth in the transition is, to greater or lesser degree, compensated if the rate of return to owners of wealth increases in the process (a likely, although not necessary outcome). For a wealth owner who plans to consume immediately after the change in regimes, an increase in the rate of return is of no value. There is no compensating gain. For one who plans to postpone consumption for a long time (for example, by passing wealth along to heirs), the gain in rate of return may more than compensate for a one-time tax.

If it were desired as a matter of policy to achieve rough neutrality in the transition—that is, generate neither gainers nor losers—it would be necessary to develop a way of discriminating among wealth owners according to their likely consumption horizons. If the distinction is based on behavior (that is, on when people actually consume), giving greater effective protection from the wealth tax on transition to those who consume (dissave) earlier, a price will be paid in the form of both equity and efficiency consequences rather at variance with the philosophical underpinnings of consumption taxation. Any attempt to discriminate with precision among people according to the timing of their planned consumption is likely to introduce such incentives, precisely because of the need to refer to people's behavior to determine their preferences.[31]

Consistent Application of Consumption-Tax Philosophy. Many people advocate a shift away from income and toward consumption taxation on grounds of efficiency. In particular, they seek the neutrality of a consumption tax (at least a uniform consumption tax) with respect to the decision to save. I have elsewhere (1986) suggested that a principal argument in favor of a consumption approach is, rather, one of equity. In brief, if two people are otherwise similarly situated but differ in their preferences in the timing of consumption, a consumption tax will impose the same burdens on them, but an income tax will discriminate in favor of the one who prefers to consume earlier. The same argument that suggests it would be unfair to discriminate between people according to their preferences for clothes of different color would imply it would be unfair to discriminate on the basis of differences in preferences for the timing of consumption.

A sketch of the way this line of argument might be carried over to policy toward transition goes as follows. Consider the two people who are similarly situated except that one prefers to postpone consumption more than the other. By the transition date, the late-consumer has a larger stock of savings than the early-consumer and will have paid more in taxes. After the transition, the two will pay the same amount of tax *except* for any wealth tax effect of the transition itself, which will work to the relative disadvantage of the late-consumer. The argument for neutrality of treatment according to preferences about the timing of consumption would seem to imply, at least, protecting the wealth in the transition. Viewed from the perspective of the lifetime treatment at the hands of the tax system, fully protecting wealth in transition leaves the discrimination against the late-consumer to the extent of the duration of the income-tax regime.

6
Concluding Remarks

There are potentially large gains to be had from pursuing what I call a consumption "strategy" of taxation. The consumption approach readily solves a variety of pesky problems in the income tax, permitting much simpler and more transparent rules in the process. I hope this study will assist in clarifying what is involved. In particular, I hope I have succeeded in showing there is less at the conceptual level to the difference from the income approach than seems often to be claimed by both advocates and opponents of the consumption approach. The difference boils down to the tax treatment of the risk-free rate of return to saving, a rate that has historically been below 1 percent per year. The rest of what is generally thought of as "capital income" is taxed alike in conceptually pure income and consumption taxes.

The existing income tax is far from "conceptually pure," however. For example, the purely inflationary element in capital gains is subjected to tax, as is the inflation premium in ordinary interest received. By the same token, the deduction for interest paid is too large by the amount of the inflation premium. There are, in addition, dozens of peculiarities in the taxation of saving and investment. The controversy over capital gains, the complex regulations governing tax-advantaged retirement savings, the double-taxation of dividends, and many other elements of the tax picture come to mind. Thus those who would defend the status quo might best divorce their arguments from the theoretical concept of income.

At the same time, the transition to the consistent consumption-type system that is within practical reach does have much in common with a shift between idealized income and consumption taxes. As described above, there is much merit in the view that the transition poses serious challenges. There seem to be two main attitudes toward those challenges. One approach is to minimize them, in the interest of moving ahead to achieve the reformers' objective. The other is to become intimidated with the problems of transition, so that they form a roadblock to change. Major tax changes have taken place (good examples in the United States include the tax reforms in 1981 and 1986) that have presumably had significant transition effects but have somehow been carried out anyway. I hope the analysis presented here will assist policy makers both to put in perspective problems of transition to consumption-based taxes and to address those that are important.

Notes

1. For useful discussions of current proposals, see U.S. Congress, Joint Committee on Taxation (1995) and Arthur Andersen (1995). A detailed description of the USA Tax, prepared by Alliance USA, was published as a special supplement by *Tax Notes*, March 10, 1995. The actual legislative proposal was reproduced as a special supplement by the Bureau of National Affairs, April 26, 1995.

2. In the helpful terminology of the Meade Committee Report (Institute for Fiscal Studies, 1978), this is an R-base ("real" transactions, as opposed to "financial") tax. There are some interesting questions about how to distinguish a financial from a real transaction. For example, is the purchase of a piece of paper giving rights to use a trademark a financial or a real transaction? Financial institutions also present special problems that I have treated elsewhere (forthcoming).

3. Throughout, the assumption is made that deductions (and credits) can be used. This would apply if losses (and net credits) were carried forward with interest, for example, or were refundable.

4. Economic differences in practice may arise because of differences in the definition of sales subject to tax—for instance, sales of clothing or medical services might be treated as taxable in one system and not in another.

5. Amounts put aside for worker retirement would also be deducted, that is, treated essentially the same as under the present income tax.

6. Particularly at higher rates of tax, it can be important to keep track of whether the tax itself is included in the calculation. So, for example, a rate of tax of 20 percent on earnings of $50,000 would produce a tax of $10,000. That amount would be 25 percent of the $40,000 consumed out of the salary by a worker who added nothing to savings during the year.

7. It is sometimes argued that the invoice-and-credit method is more easily enforced because the buyer can be required to show the tax paid by the seller; however, it would seem equally easy to trace the purchases deducted by the buyer to the tax returns of the sellers in a subtraction-method system. In contrast with the case of an income tax, there should be an inclusion on a selling business's tax return for every deduction by the buyer.

8. The general public's claim is on a share of the assets of the company, which it has helped finance through the tax deduction. The general public does not share in the reallocation of the claim through debt finance.

9. Under the U.S. income tax, *nominal* interest payments are included in the base of the recipient and deducted by the payer. Nominal interest rates include compensation for anticipated inflation and, thus, generally exceed real interest rates. For a discussion of the consequences, taking into account the presence of multiple marginal tax rates, see Bradford (1981). One of the important effects of a shift to a consumption-type tax would be automatic indexing for inflation.

10. For details on historical rates of return, see R. G. Ibbotsen Associates (1995).

11. For a related discussion, see Gordon (1985).

12. This statement applies to a tax based on accruing income, so that losses and gains are reflected immediately in the tax due. The way the deductibility of losses balances the taxation of gains was emphasized in a famous treatment by Domar and Musgrave (1944) of the effect of taxation on risk taking. Apart from problems relating to inflation, U.S. business income taxation is reasonably close to an accrual basis, although there are many exceptions. In the individual income tax, however, a "realization-based" approach complicates the story considerably. For a discussion of the complex effects of current realization-based income tax rules on incentives for risk taking, see Scarborough (1993).

13. For elaboration of this point, see Kaplow (1994).

14. It is an open question whether an actual consumption-type system would treat housing consistently with other forms of consumption.

15. Alan Tait (1991, 11–12) reports that some countries allow less than full write-off of certain capital acquisition expenses.

16. Strictly speaking, the flow of revenue to the government from a true income tax should not depend on the timing of transactions. The income calculation would be based on accruing gains and losses.

17. Even a uniform tax on a real (inflation-corrected) market-value basis has substantial implementation problems. For a discussion, see Bradford (1986). For a discussion of similar issues that arise in national income accounting, see Bradford (1991).

18. The distinction between "direct" taxes (such as income, including corporate profits, wealth, and property taxes) and "indirect" taxes, such as sales and value-added taxes, is a matter of custom and not based on any fundamental economic difference.

19. The implied measure of income of the creditor fails to satisfy the strict concept of economic income—it does not, for example, require distinguishing between interest payments and accrued interest income. It is a simple reassignment of responsibility for tax payments from the company to bondholders. For an extended discussion of the concept of economic income and why measures based on cash payments, such as interest, break down, see Bradford 1986.

20. There would be, in addition, the usual distributional effects of inflation, on fixed-income recipients, for example, or on holders of currency. See Browning (1978).

21. For a company for which equity constitutes a fraction e of the value of the company's assets, the implied percentage decline in value of the shares would be t/e, where t is the value-added tax rate. For a sufficiently leveraged firm ($e<t$), the transition incidence would imply bankruptcy (Howitt and Sinn 1989). (Note that if everyone holds the market portfolio of all financial instruments, the effect of price level change is neutralized.)

22. This is the scheme outlined in the U.S. Treasury's Comprehensive Business Income Tax plan 1992.

23. Auerbach (1989) studies the dependence of the effects of investment incentives on the cost of adjustment. See also the discussion and references in Sarkar and Zodrow (1993).

24. For further discussion of the trade-off, see Bradford et al. (1984, 180–84).

25. The same reasoning extends to the land on which owner-occupied housing sits, provided there is no tax levied on its sale. Note that I have not tried in this analysis to deal with the elimination of the property tax deduction, which is not related to the choice between income- and consumption-tax regimes.

26. Hall and Rabushka (1995) advocate this form of transition to the flat tax.

27. Although I do not develop the point here, it might be noted that a similar line of argument leads to the conclusion that to pro-

tect old savings from the one-time tax on transition to a consumed-income tax at the personal level would involve allowing immediate recovery of basis.

28. To establish whether these conditions are fulfilled in fact, and whether a particular transition plan would effect such a general gain, would require more detailed empirical analysis than has been carried out to date.

29. Taking into account risk leads to an interesting modification of this story.

30. I have particularly benefited from discussions with Louis Kaplow on the subject of this section. Some of his ideas about transitions in general are set out in Kaplow (1986) and about transition to a consumption-type tax in Kaplow (1995).

31. This point is emphasized by Kaplow (1995) in his analysis of the USA tax. The USA tax proposal incorporates a system for individuals to recover the basis in their wealth at the time of transition, but the recovery is postponed until such time as the taxpayer becomes a net dissaver.

References

Alliance USA. "USA Tax System." *Tax Notes*, Special supplement 66, no. 11, March 10, 1995.

Arthur Andersen. Office of Federal Tax Services, "Tax Reform 1995: Looking at Two Options." Arthur Andersen & Co., SC, May 1995.

Auerbach, Alan J. "Tax Reform and Adjustment Costs: The Impact on Investment and Market Value." *International Economic Review* (1989): 939–62.

Auerbach, Alan J., Jagadeesh Gokhale, and Laurence J. Kotlikoff. "Generational Accounting: A Meaningful Way to Evaluate Fiscal Policy." *Journal of Economic Perspectives* 7 (1993).

Auerbach, Alan J., and Laurence J. Kotlikoff. "National Savings, Economic Welfare, and the Structure of Taxation." In *Behavioral Simulation Methods in Tax Policy Analysis,* edited by Martin Feldstein. Chicago: University of Chicago Press, 1983.

———. *Dynamic Fiscal Policy.* New York: Cambridge University Press, 1987.

Bradford, David F. "Issues in the Design of Savings and Investment Incentives." In *Depreciation, Inflation and the Taxation of Income from Capital,* edited by Charles R. Hulten, 13–47. Washington, D.C.: Urban Institute, 1981.

————. *Untangling the Income Tax.* Cambridge, Mass.: Harvard University Press, 1986.

————. "On the Incidence of Consumption Taxes." In *The Consumption Tax: A Better Alternative,* edited by Charls E. Walker and Mark A. Bloomfield, 243–61. Cambridge, Mass.: Ballinger, 1987.

————. "What Are Consumption Taxes and Who Bears Them?" *Tax Notes,* April 18, 1988.

————. "Market Value versus Financial Accounting Measures of National Saving." In *National Saving and Economic Performance,* edited by B. Douglas Bernheim and John B. Shoven, 15–44. Chicago: University of Chicago Press, 1991.

————. "Treatment of Financial Services under Income and Consumption Taxes." In *Economic Effects of Fundamental Tax Reform.* Edited by Henry Aaron and William Gale. 1996, Washington, D.C.: Brookings Institution, forthcoming.

Bradford, David F., and the U.S. Treasury Tax Policy Staff. *Blueprints for Basic Tax Reform,* 2d ed., rev. Arlington, Va.: Tax Analysts, 1984.

Browning, Edgar K. "The Burden of Taxation." *Journal of Political Economy* 86 (August 1978): 649–71.

Bureau of National Affairs. "USA Tax Act of 1995." Special supplement, report no. 80, April 26, 1995.

Domar, Evsey D., and Richard Musgrave. "Proportional Income Taxation and Risk Bearing." *Quarterly Journal of Economics* 58 (1944): 382–482.

Gordon, Roger H. "Taxation of Corporate Capital Income: Tax Revenues versus Tax Distortions." *Quarterly Journal of Economics* 100 (February 1985): 1–27.

Hall, Robert E., and Alvin Rabushka. *Low Tax, Simple Tax, Flat Tax.* New York: McGraw-Hill, 1983.

————. *The Flat Tax.* 2d ed. Stanford, Calif.: Hoover Institution Press, 1995.

Howitt, Peter, and Hans-Werner Sinn. "Gradual Reforms of Capital Income Taxation." *American Economic Re-*

view 79 (1989): 106–24.

Institute for Fiscal Studies. *The Structure and Reform of Direct Taxation: The Report of a Committee Chaired by Professor J. E. Meade.* London: George Allen & Unwin, 1978.

Jorgenson, Dale W. "The Economic Impact of Fundamental Tax Reform." Paper presented at the Hoover Institution Conference on Frontiers of Tax Reform, Washington, D.C., May 11, 1995.

Kaplow, Louis. "An Economic Analysis of Legal Transitions." *Harvard Law Review* (January 1986).

———. "Taxation and Risk Taking: A General Equilibrium Perspective." *National Tax Journal* 47, no. 4 (December 1994): 789–98.

———. "Recovery of Pre-Transition Basis under an Individual Consumption Tax: The USA Tax System." *Tax Notes*, August 28, 1995.

Keuschnigg, Christian. "The Transition to a Cash Flow Income Tax." *Swiss Journal of Economics and Statistics* 127, no. 2 (1991): 113–40.

Kotlikoff, Laurence J. *Generational Accounting: Knowing Who Pays, and When, for What We Spend.* New York: Free Press, 1992.

R. G. Ibbotsen Associates. *Stocks, Bonds, Bills and Inflation: 1995 Yearbook.* Chicago, 1995.

Sarkar, Shounak, and George R. Zodrow. "Transitional Issues in Moving to a Direct Consumption Tax." *National Tax Journal*, 46, no. 3 (September 1993): 359–76.

Scarborough, Robert H. "Risk, Diversification and the Design of Loss Limitations under a Realization-based Income Tax." *Tax Law Review* 48, no. 3 (1993): 677–717.

Summers, Lawrence H. "Capital Taxation and Accumulation in a Life Cycle Growth Model." *American Economic Review* 71 (September 1981): 533–44.

Tait, Alan A., ed. *Value-added Tax: Administrative and*

Policy Issues. Washington, D.C.: International Monetary Fund, October 1991.

U.S. Congress, Joint Committee on Taxation. *Discussion of Issues Relating to "Flat" Tax Rate Proposals* (JCS-7-95). Washington, D.C.: U.S. Government Printing Office, 1995.

U.S. Treasury Department. *Blueprints for Basic Tax Reform*. Washington, D.C.: U.S. Government Printing Office, January 1977.

————. *Report on Integration of Individual and Corporate Tax Systems: Taxing Business Income Once*. Washington, D.C.: U.S. Government Printing Office, January 1992.

About the Author

DAVID F. BRADFORD is professor of economics and public affairs at the Woodrow Wilson School of Public and International Affairs, Princeton University, and adjunct professor of law at New York University. He is an adjunct scholar of the American Enterprise Institute and a research associate of the National Bureau of Economic Research. Mr. Bradford was a member of the President's Council of Economic Advisers from 1991 to 1993 and was the deputy assistant secretary for tax policy at the Treasury Department from 1975 to 1977.

He is the author of several publications on tax policy, including (with the U.S. Treasury Tax Policy Staff) *Blueprints for Basic Reform* (second edition, 1984) and *Untangling the Income Tax* (1986). He is the editor of *Distributional Analysis of Tax Policy* (AEI Press, 1995) and coauthor, with Derrick A. Max, of *Intergenerational Transfers under Community Rating* (AEI Press, 1996).

AEI STUDIES ON TAX REFORM
R. Glenn Hubbard and Diana Furchtgott-Roth
series editors

ASSESSING THE EFFECTIVENESS OF SAVING INCENTIVES
R. Glenn Hubbard and Jonathan S. Skinner

FUNDAMENTAL ISSUES IN CONSUMPTION TAXATION
David F. Bradford

www.ingramcontent.com/pod-product-compliance
Lightning Source LLC
Jackson TN
JSHW011943131224
75386JS00041B/1529